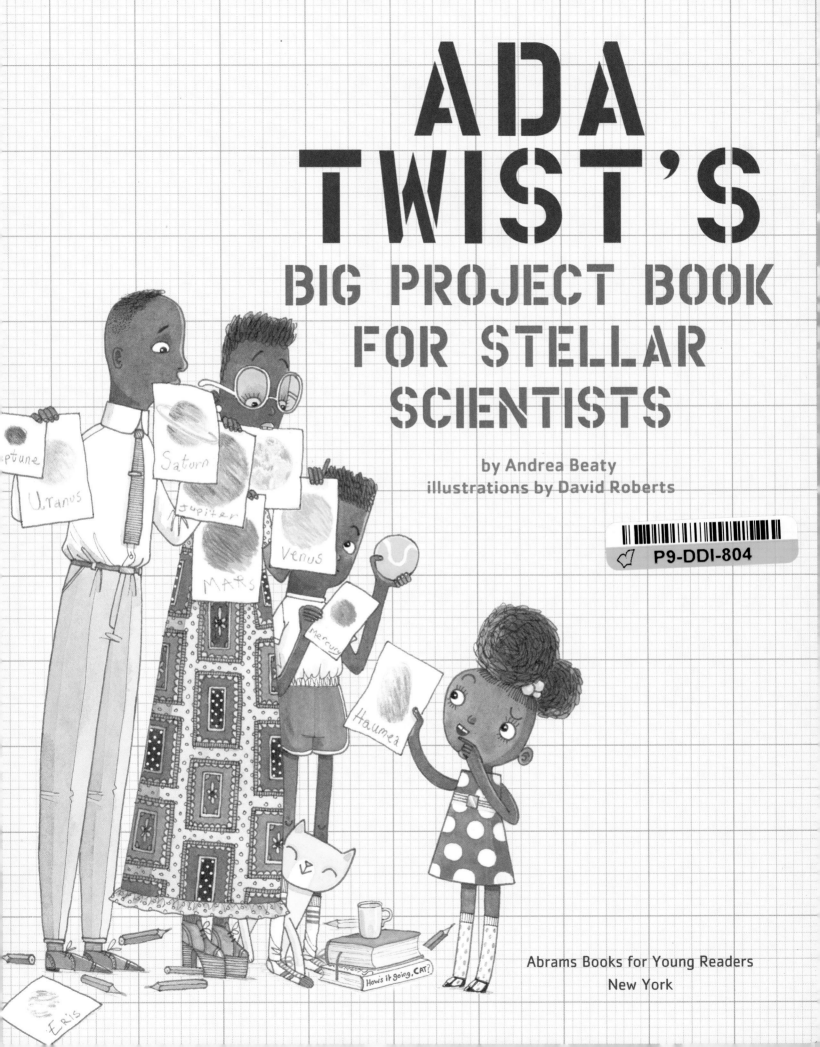

ADA TWIST'S
BIG PROJECT BOOK FOR STELLAR SCIENTISTS

by Andrea Beaty

illustrations by David Roberts

P9-DDI-804

Abrams Books for Young Readers
New York

There are many kinds of scientists.
They study earth and sky,
plant and ocean, rock and star,
bug and butterfly.
And yet, they share the same pursuit:
To ask the question, "Why?"

Cataloging-in-Publication Data has been applied for and may be obtained from the Library of Congress.

ISBN 978-1-4197-3024-5

Text copyright © 2018 Andrea Beaty
Illustrations copyright © 2018 David Roberts
Instructional illustrations by Noah MacMillan
Book design by Chad W. Beckerman and Laura Crescenti

Printed and bound in U.S.A.
10 9 8 7 6 5 4 3 2 1

Abrams Books for Young Readers are available at special discounts when purchased in quantity for premiums and promotions as well as fundraising or educational use. Special editions can also be created to specification. For details, contact specialsales@abramsbooks.com or the address below.

Pages 19, 20: iStock.com/Antagain. Page 34: iStock.com/sololos. Page 35: iStock.com/olegkalina. Page 42 (*top left*) Hayat Sindi-PopTech 2012-Camden Maine USA copyright © 2012 Thatcher Cook for PopTech, provided under Creative Commons Attribution-ShareAlike 2.0 Generic license, flickr.com/photos/40287103@N07/8103609979; (*middle left*) © David Rose/Telegraph Media Group Limited 2009; (*bottom right*) The Green Belt Movement. Page 45: iStock.com/DCorn. Pages 56, 57: iStock.com/alanphillips. Page 72: iStock.com/pmstephens. Page 88: Pitch drop experiment with John Mainstone copyright © 2007 University of Queensland, provided under Creative Commons Attribution-ShareAlike 3.0 Unported license, upload.wikimedia.org/wikipedia/commons/0/03/Pitch_drop_experiment_with_John_Mainstone.jpg.

ABRAMS The Art of Books
195 Broadway, New York, NY 10007
abramsbooks.com

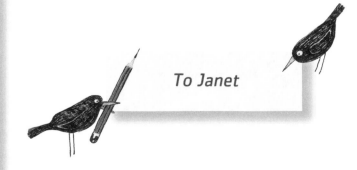

To Janet

CONGRATULATIONS! YOU ARE A SCIENTIST JUST LIKE ADA TWIST!

This book is a tool to help you become an even better scientist! Use the blank spaces for your ideas. Imagine. Draw pictures. Ask questions. Create. Doodle!

Have fun exploring your scientific ideas and questions and your dreams. You can share your creations with others or keep this project book all to yourself. You decide.

This book is for **YOU!**

World's Greatest Scientist

Your name here:
_____

Your picture here:

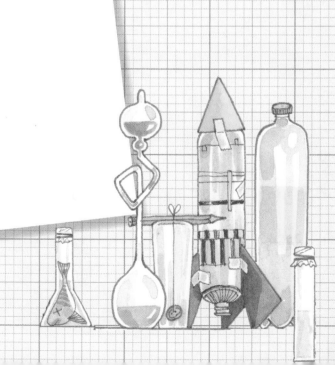

THE STORY OF ADA TWIST, SCIENTIST

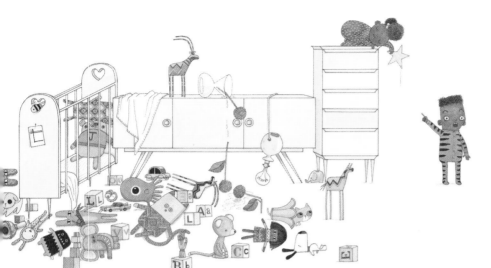

Ada Marie Twist was a quiet but curious baby. One day, she piled up her stuffed bears and broke out of her crib. Ada was on the go! She tore through her room exploring everything, and she didn't stop until she conked out at night.

Her frazzled parents did their best to keep up with Ada as she explored the world. They worried a little that she did not speak even as she grew older, but they could see that she was always thinking and figured she would start talking when she had something to say.

That's just what happened when Ada turned three. She climbed to the tip-top of the grandfather clock to see what was there.

"STOP!" yelled her parents.

Ada stopped. Her chin quivered. She took a deep breath. And for the first time, Ada spoke.

"Why?" she asked.

That was it. Once Ada started asking questions,
she did not stop!

"Why does it tick and why does it tock?"

"Why don't we call it a granddaughter clock?"

"Why are there pointy things stuck to a rose?"

"Why are there hairs up inside of your nose?"

Why? What? How? When? She asked over and over
and over again! Ada wanted to know EVERYTHING.
As she drifted to sleep after a long day of questions,
her parents smiled and whispered,
"You'll figure it out."

As Ada got older, her parents tried their best to help her find answers to
her many questions. Even Miss Lila Greer found that her hands were quite
full as Ada performed wonderful but rather messy experiments at school.
It was very clear that Ada Twist was a scientist.

On the first day of spring, Ada was busy with an experiment. She was testing the sounds that make mockingbirds sing when—*ZOWIE!*—a terrible stench whacked her in the nose!

What kind of stink could make her toes curl like that? Ada Twist had to find out.

First, Ada researched smelling and smells.

Next, Ada came up with a hypothesis, an idea she thought could explain the terrible stink. Ada wondered if that horrifying stink came from her father's cabbage stew. She tested her hypothesis, but she concluded that the stew did not explain the terrible stink.

She came up with hypothesis two: The cat made the stink.

However, the cat needed some help making such a big stink. Ada sprayed the cat with her mother's fancy perfume and her father's cologne. It made the cat stink, but it was not the stink that made her toes curl. Hypothesis two was proven wrong.

Ada needed to start again, but first she had to clean the cat. Ada Marie Twist started to do something that nobody should EVER do! She tried to give the cat a bath in the washing machine. It was a terrible idea! An awful idea! A horrible idea! And boy, did she get in trouble.

So she sat and sat and sat. And she thought about science and stink and the cat. And how experiments made so much mess.

Ada wondered so many things. And then she wondered once more what made that terrible stink. She scribbled a thought on the wall. Then she scribbled another. And another. And ANOTHER.

Her parents calmed down and came back to talk. They looked at the hall, and they were shocked. Ada had scribbled her questions and thoughts on the entire wall.

What would they do with this curious child who wanted to know what the world was about?

They kissed her and whispered, "We'll figure it out."

After that day, Ada's family got in the act of helping young Ada sort fiction from fact. And all her friends in grade two helped. Perhaps one day, they will discover the source of that terrible stink that curls toes!

Ada collects all kinds of things for her scientific experiments. Here are some things she finds useful. She calls these items her

"SCIENTIST'S TREASURE."

You might find them useful, too. What items would you include?

Clean tin cans

Aluminum foil

Plastic wrap

Colored paper

Straws

Measuring cups

Measuring spoons

Muffin baking tin

Rulers

Scale

Magnifying glass

Mirror

String

Notebooks

Science books

ENGINEERING

Hand trowel

Pail

Test tubes and flasks

Sharpie markers

Paper egg carton

Toothpicks

Tape

Post-it notes

Scissors

Goggles or safety glasses

Rubber gloves

Eyedropper

Tweezers

Seeds

Potting soil

Paper towels

Thermometer

Kitchen timer

Rubber bands

Vinegar

Baking soda

Pens and pencils

SODA LUX

Baking dish

Clean, empty food containers

Plastic garbage bags

Where can **you** find SCIENTIST'S TREASURE?

There are many places you can find cool things to use in your experiments.

- RECYCLING: Cardboard boxes, broken toys, juice cans, milk jugs, plastic lids, and other things your family might otherwise throw away. Ask permission and make sure they're clean and safe to use.

- RUMMAGE SALES and THRIFT STORES are great places to find useful items inexpensively. Finding a new use for something old keeps it out of the landfill!

- SWAP treasure with your scientist friends.

- If you can't find a recycled thing to use, you might find something at a HARDWARE STORE or a FABRIC STORE.

AND BE CAREFUL WHEN WORKING WITH SHARP TOOLS OR BROKEN PIECES! MAKE SURE AN ADULT IS ALWAYS NEARBY!

KEEP YOUR SCIENTIST'S TREASURE ORGANIZED!

Treasure is all around. But not everything is a treasure.
Choose items that are safe, clean, and useful.

A good collection has variety and is well organized.

ORGANIZING YOUR TOOLS AND TREASURE . . .

- keeps them in good shape, so they last longer.
- lets you find what you need when you need it.
- saves money, because you don't have to replace things you already have.
- keeps your space clean so you can conduct experiments.
- keeps your feet free of holes!

HERE ARE SOME TIPS:

- Decorate and label empty shoeboxes to store under your bed or on a shelf.

- Keep similar things together.

- Small, clean glass jars with lids make great containers for tiny parts like screws and bolts or supplies like rubber bands and string. Clear jars let you easily see what you have!

- A clear plastic shoe holder over the back of a door keeps things organized and easily viewed.

- Hang tools on hooks on a peg board from the hardware store.

- Magnetic strips from the hardware store or sewing store can hold metal scissors and other metal tools.

- An empty can makes a great holder for tools. You can decorate the can. Watch out for sharp edges! Wrap it in decorative paper and ribbon.

Always be safe when you are conducting experiments. Protect your eyes with safety glasses.

A scientist is always careful!

Don't forget these!

What special things will you add to your **SCIENTIST'S TREASURE**?

_____

_____

_____

_____

_____

_____

_____

_____

_____

_____

_____

_____

_____

_____

_____

_____

_____

_____

SCIENTISTS USE SPECIAL TOOLS.

Scopes are tools that let scientists look at things more clearly. Telescopes show us large things that are very far away. Microscopes show us very small things that are close to us. Periscopes let submarines look around above the water.

Fill a bucket with water and toss in a variety of coins or small plastic toys. How clearly can you see the items through the water? Water is often difficult to see through because its surface reflects light and distorts the view. Build a simple aquascope to help you see through the water.

MATERIALS:

Can opener

Clean, empty food can

Plastic wrap

Scissors

Large rubber bands

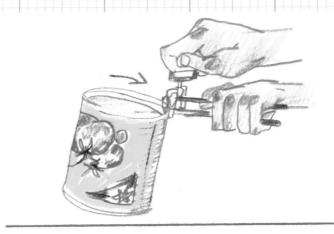

1. Using a can opener, carefully remove the bottom of the empty can.

2. Put the can on one end on a flat surface, like a table.

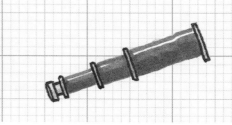

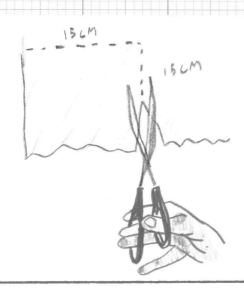

3. Cut a piece of plastic wrap 15 cm x 15 cm with the scissors.

4. Place the plastic wrap over the top of the can.

5. Smooth the plastic wrap down over the can. Make sure to keep the plastic wrap wrinkle-free.

6. Secure the plastic wrap with rubber bands.

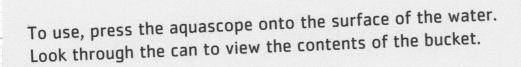

To use, press the aquascope onto the surface of the water. Look through the can to view the contents of the bucket.

THE SCIENCES

Like all scientists, Ada Twist is curious! There are so many branches of science she can investigate. Some explore the planets. Some focus on physical motion. Some look at life on earth. Others delve into the smallest particles of the atoms that make up everything. Some branches of science combine two or more of these!

Here are just a few of the kinds of science you might explore like Ada Twist.

PHYSICAL SCIENCES study natural objects that are not alive.

PHYSICS—motion, heat, energy, light, sound, and the structure of atoms

CHEMISTRY—matter (what stuff is made of), its properties, and how it interacts with other matter and energy

ASTRONOMY—the whole physical universe and the space and objects in it

GEOLOGY—the physical structure of the earth and the processes that change it

BIOLOGICAL SCIENCES

study things that are alive—or that once were.

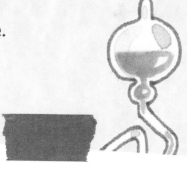

BOTANY—plants

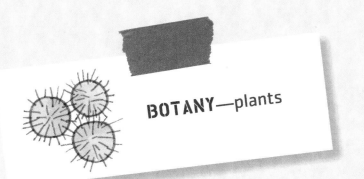

ZOOLOGY—animals

MICROBIOLOGY—microorganisms, the forms of life that are so tiny you can't see them with only your eyes

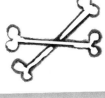

PHYSIOLOGY—the function and structure of living organisms

PALEONTOLOGY—fossils of animals and plants. How plants and animals evolve over time.

NEUROBIOLOGY— the human brain. How it works to learn new things and forget old ones, and how thinking thoughts works.

GENETICS—heredity and how parents pass traits to their offspring

SCIENTIST'S WORD SEARCH

Can you find all the words listed to the right in the puzzle below?

(In case you need help, the answer key can be found on page 94.)

```
B T K A N H P Q R T A C I O N J
O C P S G I N D U S T R I B L E
T A H A K T S X O T B V E S M E
A P Y E C O L O G Y A C T E E I
N O S C M T O P T I C A L R T W
Y W I E H I M L E E N V I V E N
I E C L A B S E I V X M C A O R
M J S S U R T T I E R W A T R V
A W P C E J K E R N A O Z I O O
L M Z T P R V S C Y O U L O L D
M I C R O B I O L O G Y H N O I
L P B O Y I O R Z R U I K O G D
Q H Y P O T H E S I S R N Q Y M
V E I I Q M E D I C I N E G M A
A A U C X G G R E M U M D L M Y
Y U B I O L O G Y E C T R I C A
```

14

BOTANY	OCEANOGRAPHY	MICROBIOLOGY	OBSERVATION
BIOLOGY	ASTRONOMY	PALEONTOLOGY	MEASUREMENT
CHEMISTRY	METEOROLOGY	ECOLOGY	QUANTIFY
PHYSICS	ZOOLOGY	HYPOTHESIS	FACT
GEOLOGY	MEDICINE	TEST	

```
R  C  T  T  S  O  V  T  W  M  S  R  A  N  B
A  G  R  E  C  U  L  F  U  R  A  P  S  U  L
A  T  R  S  N  I  C  A  K  T  T  A  T  A  V
J  L  M  T  N  S  S  C  O  K  E  L  R  S  E
A  F  Q  H  K  M  I  T  M  K  C  E  O  R  I
C  T  A  L  V  M  G  Q  U  I  G  O  N  U  U
M  E  A  S  U  R  E  M  E  N  T  N  O  X  E
O  F  A  U  H  N  H  A  U  N  T  T  M  O  U
Q  I  C  N  L  N  H  L  I  F  V  O  Y  F  H
C  U  I  Z  O  O  L  O  G  Y  S  L  R  T  N
L  I  A  D  E  G  N  S  T  H  E  O  M  A  T
U  P  I  N  T  E  R  M  X  R  V  G  J  O  B
W  E  L  E  T  C  S  A  M  Q  E  Y  B  G  F
N  E  M  N  E  I  E  R  P  S  P  A  C  E  Y
F  N  A  R  I  V  F  R  F  H  V  S  N  Y  Z
I  G  E  O  L  O  G  Y  I  A  Y  S  D  A  N
```

SCIENTISTS ARE CURIOUS.

Scientists look at the world around them and wonder why and how.
Each question brings up more questions. Sometimes, like branches
of a tree, the questions get more and more refined and detailed.
Can you create a question tree? What would you like to know about?

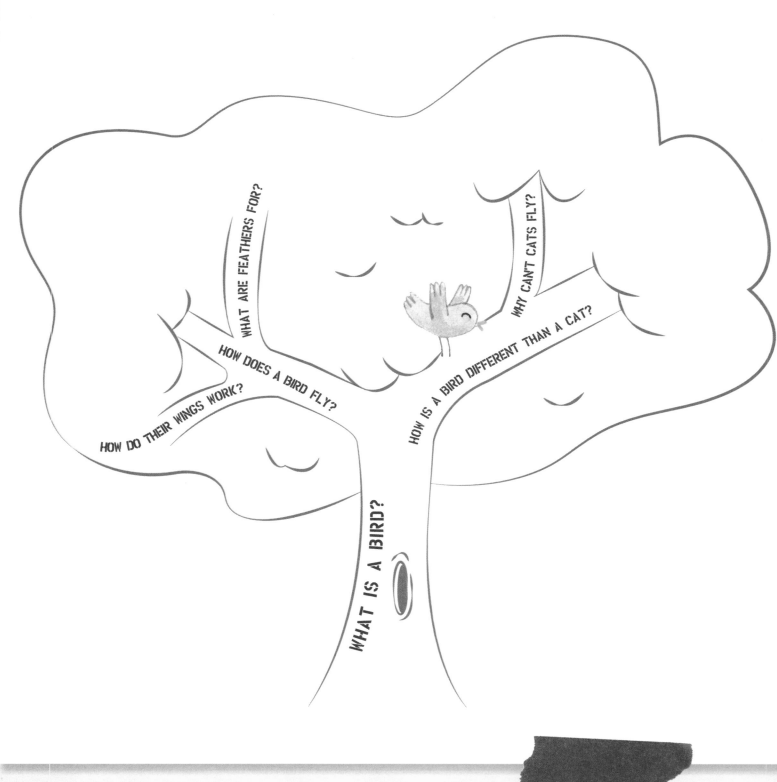

Ada Marie did what scientists do.

She asked a small question, and then she asked two.

And each of those led her to three questions more.

Some of those questions resulted in four.

AS A MATTER OF FACT . . .

Is that a fact?

What does a fact do?

It helps us determine

what's false and what's true.

A fact isn't made up

or what we might feel.

A fact can be proven

and that makes it real.

Sorting fiction and feelings from fact is what scientists do!

A fact is a bit of information that can be proven. A fact is a fact is a fact, even if someone says it is not. Scientists try to sort fiction from fact through research and testing.

Fiction is story. Stories help us understand the world around us. They also help us understand ourselves and each other, which is why they are so powerful. Stories can give us strong feelings. Stories can include facts, but stories are not facts.

Feelings are emotions. We use feelings to react to the world around us. We can feel happy, sad, angry, hungry, silly, worried, and excited. We can have lots of feelings at the same time. Feelings are one of the best parts of being human. But feelings are not facts and they do not change facts.

Can you help Ada and her friends sort fact from fiction? And from feelings?

LADYBUG FACTS

THE FACTS:

These facts have been researched from the Britannica Library Reference Center, which is a reliable source. A librarian or teacher can help you figure out if a source can be trusted.

Ladybugs are also called "ladybird beetles." There are about 5,000 species (kinds) of ladybugs. Their scientific family name is *Coccinellidae*. They vary in looks but usually are brightly colored with spots or markings. Most ladybugs are carnivorous, which means that they eat other animals. They especially eat aphids and mites and scales that are pests to crops. That makes the ladybugs useful in agriculture. However, there are at least two kinds of ladybugs (*Epilachna borealis* and *Epilachna varivestis*) that eat plants and are considered pests by farmers.

Ladybugs have six legs. They also have a pair of antennae and two sets of wings. The hard outer wings are called elytra, and they protect the other pair, which unfold for flight.

THINK ABOUT THESE STATEMENTS. ARE THEY FACTS? ARE THEY FICTION? ARE THEY FEELINGS? CROSS OUT ANYTHING THAT IS NOT A PROVEN FACT.

- There are 27 ladybugs.

- There are 30 ladybugs.

- Ladybugs are dangerous.

- The outer wings are called the elytra.

- Ladybugs make people happy.

- Ladybugs can fly.

- Ladybugs prefer to drive.

- Ladybugs eat frogs.

- Ada Twist loves ladybugs.

- Frogs eat ladybugs.

- Ladybugs are pests.

- Ladybugs are from the family *Cornucopia*.

- Some ladybugs are agricultural pests.

- Ladybugs are lucky.

- Ladybugs have eight legs.

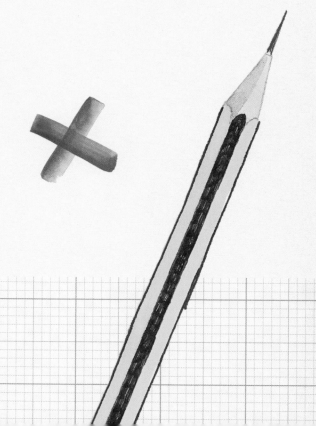

SCIENTISTS THINK.

Scientists are critical thinkers. They ask questions, do research, and think carefully about what they learn.

Scientists research topics to learn all they can. First they look for good resources. Libraries are great places to seek facts.

Use a reference book or a book from the library to find facts about your favorite animal. If you need help, ask a librarian!

Record your findings here:

_____

_____

_____

_____

_____

_____

_____

_____

_____

_____

_____

_____

_____

_____

_____

_____

SCIENTISTS KEEP THINKING.

They don't quit thinking about something after they have found an answer. Scientists ask more questions and dig deeper to find more answers.

After researching your favorite animal, do you have new questions?

List them here:

_____

_____

_____

_____

_____

_____

_____

_____

READ. QUESTION. THINK. THAT'S HOW SCIENTISTS GET THINGS DONE!

THE SCIENTIFIC METHOD

Scientists use the **SCIENTIFIC METHOD** to think clearly about a question and seek answers in a logical way.

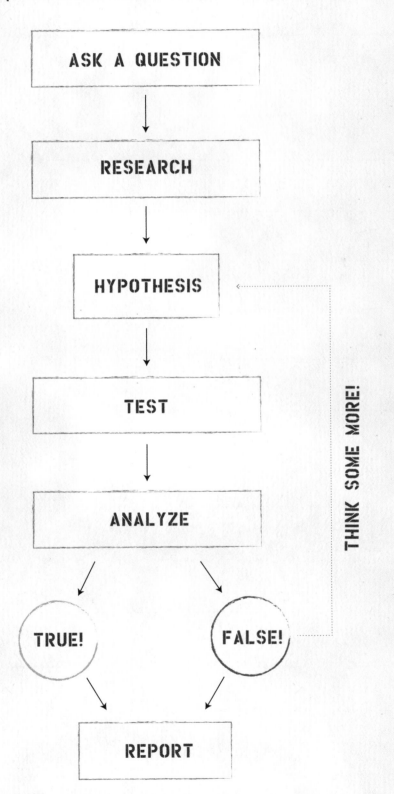

Here is how Ada Twist used the scientific method to try to figure out what caused the terrible stink that whacked her in the nose:

1. She asked a question: What was the source of that terrible stink?

2. Ada researched all that she could about smelling and smells, both the stinky and the good.

3. Ada came up with a hypothesis that her father's cabbage stew, with its stinky dead fish, lots of garlic, onions, and other specific smelly ingredients, created the pungent aroma that curled up her toes.

4. Ada tested her hypothesis and observed the results.

5. She analyzed her results and found that the hypothesis was false.

6. She thought up a different hypothesis and then tested it.

7. She discussed her findings with her family.

SCIENTISTS ARE OBSERVANT.

They pay attention to tiny and big details.

It's easy to look at things without learning from them.
Here are some ways to be a better observer:

I. KEEP NOTES.
A small field notebook and pencil can help you do that.

2. BE SPECIFIC ABOUT THE SETTING.
Record the time of day, location, temperature, and any other factors that might change and affect your research.

3. USE SPECIFIC MEASUREMENTS IN YOUR NOTES WHEN POSSIBLE.
Saying "a one centimeter (1 cm) long beetle" is more helpful than saying "a big beetle."

4. DRAW PICTURES WHEN POSSIBLE.
Then add them to your data (information).

When scientists observe, they think about what they see, hear, taste, touch, and smell, and they gather as many details as possible. Use your senses to gather data.

At lunch or dinner, gather details about what you are eating. Be specific. Quantify (count or measure) what you find when possible. Think about each of your senses. Use the questions below to help get you started.

TASTE · SMELL · TOUCH · SIGHT · SOUND

What are you eating? How much? What colors? Shapes? Sizes? Flavors? Textures? Sounds? Smells?

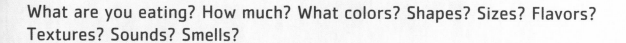

Make detailed notes about your meal here:

_____

_____

_____

_____

_____

_____

_____

_____

Draw and label a picture of your meal here:

STOP AND OBSERVE!

Look around you right now. What do you observe?
Focus on just one object you see.

Make detailed notes or pictures. Think about what it feels like,
its sound, size, and color, the materials in it, its purpose . . .

Think of three questions about that thing. Write them here.
If you can't think of any questions, wait a bit. They will come
along! Think about how, when, where, why . . .

Try again. For each question, think of two more!

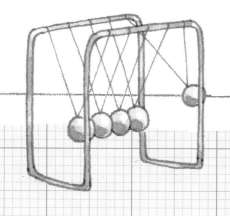

WATCH THE NIGHT SKY
WITH ADA TWIST

Ada went outside one night and looked up at the sky. It was vast and beautiful.
It filled her with wonder . . . and questions.

HOW FAR AWAY ARE THE STARS?

Stars are distant suns just like our sun. The next closest star is called Proxima Centauri and is 40,208,000,000,000 kilometers or 25,000,000,000,000 (25 trillion!) miles from the earth. If you traveled there at the speed of light, it would take a little more than four years. Pack a lunch!

WHY DO STARS TWINKLE?

Stars twinkle because they are so VERY far away that their light reaches the earth as a single beam that bounces around a little in the earth's atmosphere before it reaches our eyes. That bouncing makes the star seem brighter, then dimmer, then brighter. That is the twinkling we see.

WHY *DON'T* SOME STARS TWINKLE?

They don't twinkle because they are planets! They look like stars in the night sky because they reflect the light of our sun. But planets are much, much closer than any stars. The light they reflect hits our atmosphere as many small beams of light. While the individual beams also bounce around in our atmosphere, there are lots of them so our eyes do not notice the bouncing . . . and we see the planets as non-twinkling lights.

WHAT ARE THE BLINKING LIGHTS TRAVELING THROUGH THE SKY?

Those are high-flying airplanes!

WHAT ARE THE LIGHTS THAT STREAK ACROSS THE SKY, THEN GO OUT?

Those are shooting stars. Shooting stars aren't stars at all. They are chunks of rock called meteors that burn up when they hit the earth's atmosphere. They almost always burn completely away in the atmosphere, but sometimes a tiny bit of a meteor makes it through the atmosphere and lands on the earth! Sometimes, a large group of meteors will pass the earth together. This event of many shooting stars together is called a meteor shower. It is much nicer to watch than a meteor bath.

WHAT ARE THE LIGHTS TRAVELING FAST IN STRAIGHT LINES ACROSS THE SKY?

Those are satellites that orbit the earth, reflecting the light of the sun as they go. One of them might even be the International Space Station, which orbits the earth every 92 minutes. It travels at 28,000 kilometers per hour or 17,500 miles per hour. That's fast!

WHAT DO YOU SEE IN THE NIGHT SKY?

When you get the chance, go to a dark place and look at the night sky.

List what you see here. Write questions that you have as well.

You will have the best viewing far from city lights. You will see different objects depending upon when and where you watch the sky. Add to your list every time you get to look up.

LOOK UP AT THE NIGHT SKY

Each of the stars you see is a sun like ours, but is very, very, VERY far away.
Can you imagine a planet orbiting a distant sun? Is it like our planet?
Is it different? What would you name your planet?

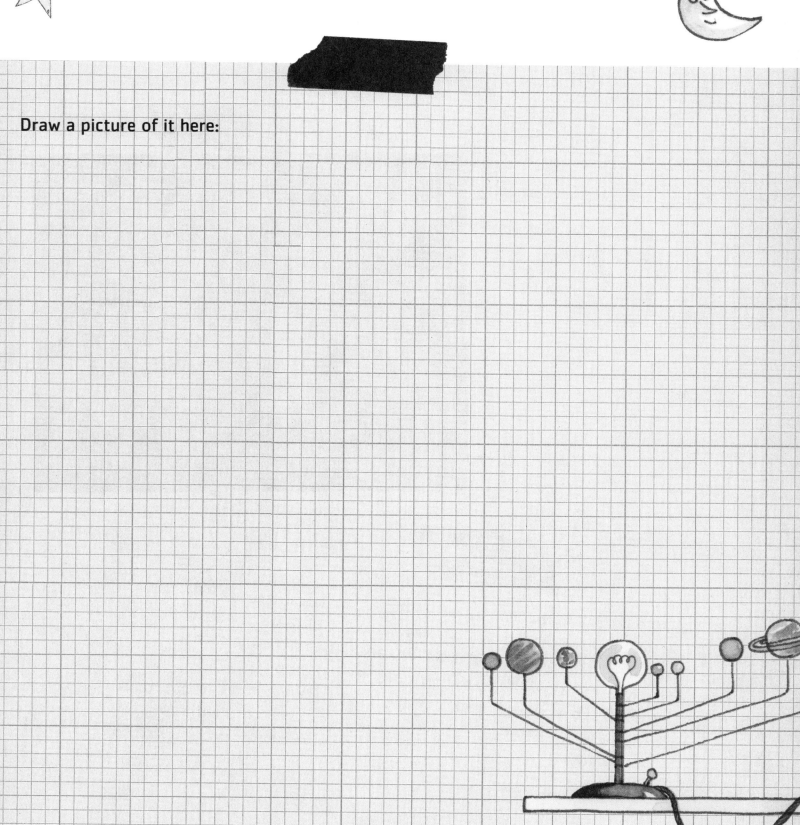

Draw a picture of it here:

CONSTELLATIONS

Humans have combined their stories with maps of the stars throughout history. These patterns in the stars are called constellations, and they helped travelers navigate oceans and deserts and unknown lands. Each culture brought its own stories to the stars.

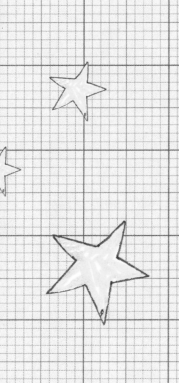

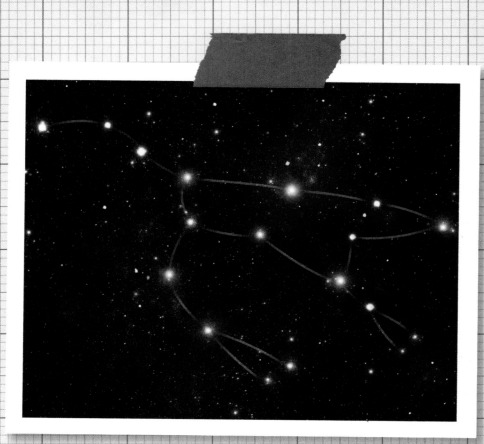

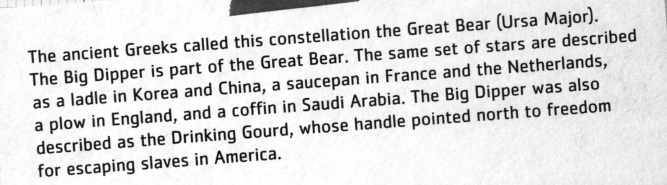

The ancient Greeks called this constellation the Great Bear (Ursa Major). The Big Dipper is part of the Great Bear. The same set of stars are described as a ladle in Korea and China, a saucepan in France and the Netherlands, a plow in England, and a coffin in Saudi Arabia. The Big Dipper was also described as the Drinking Gourd, whose handle pointed north to freedom for escaping slaves in America.

Constellations are just bunches of stars that humans grouped together. This let people feel connected to the stars through story. They also act as road maps for astronomers and navigators studying the stars.

Look at this picture of the sky. Connect some of the stars to create a pattern and write a short story about it.

_____

_____

_____

_____

WHY DOES THE MOON CHANGE SHAPE?

Or does it?

The moon does not change, but we can't always see all of it. Since the moon does not make its own light, we can only see it when it reflects the sun's light. The amount of the moon we can see depends upon its position compared to the sun and the earth. The moon is always in motion as it orbits around the earth while the earth is always in motion orbiting the sun.

When the part of the moon we can see is growing larger each night, we say that it is *waxing*. When the moon is completely visible, it is a full moon. After that, we see less of the moon each night. That is called *waning*.

A crescent moon is just a sliver of the moon and a gibbous moon is almost completely full.

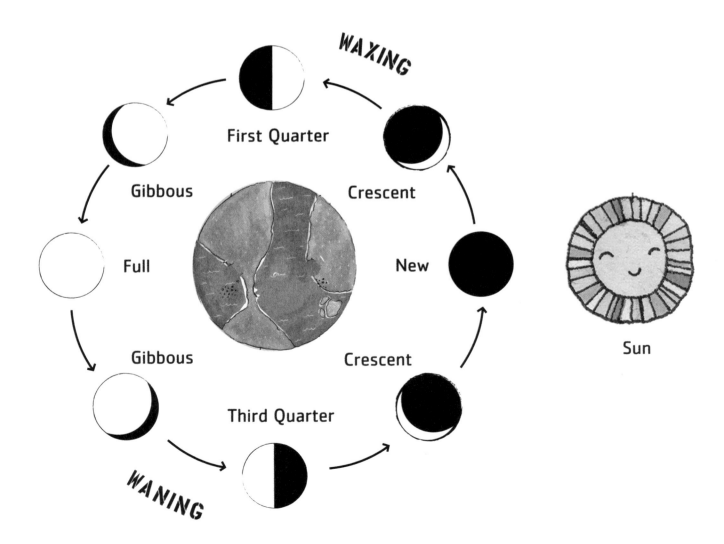

WAXING

First Quarter

Gibbous

Crescent

Full

New

Gibbous

Crescent

Third Quarter

WANING

Sun

Keep a journal of the moon for one month. Draw the shape of the moon as you see it. How does it change? Why does it change?

SUNDAY	MONDAY	TUESDAY	WEDNESDAY	THURSDAY	FRIDAY	SATURDAY
◯	◯	◯	◯	◯	◯	◯
◯	◯	◯	◯	◯	◯	◯
◯	◯	◯	◯	◯	◯	◯
◯	◯	◯	◯	◯	◯	◯
◯	◯	◯	◯	◯	◯	◯

Time for you to collect some data.
Use a ruler to measure three things.
Draw them here and record their length.

To quantify, what must you do?

You find how many or how few.

How slow. How fast.

How short. How tall.

You don't count some. You count them all.

Gather data. Find the facts.

When you're done, you can relax.

What else can you quantify? Here are some ideas:

• Count the number of shoes, plates, eggs, or books in your house.

• When you are in a car, ask the driver to tell you how fast the car is traveling.

• Get a glass of water. Pour it into a measuring cup to measure how much water the glass contained.

Scientists collect data. As scientists perform experiments, they try to collect information that is accurate so they can get the most usable results.

To do this, they take and record detailed measurements.

SCIENTISTS USE DETAILS TO DESCRIBE THINGS.

Work with a friend. Take turns drawing a simple object by filling in the cubes on the grid below. Describe the drawing as accurately as you can to your friend, who will try to draw it on a piece of graph paper.

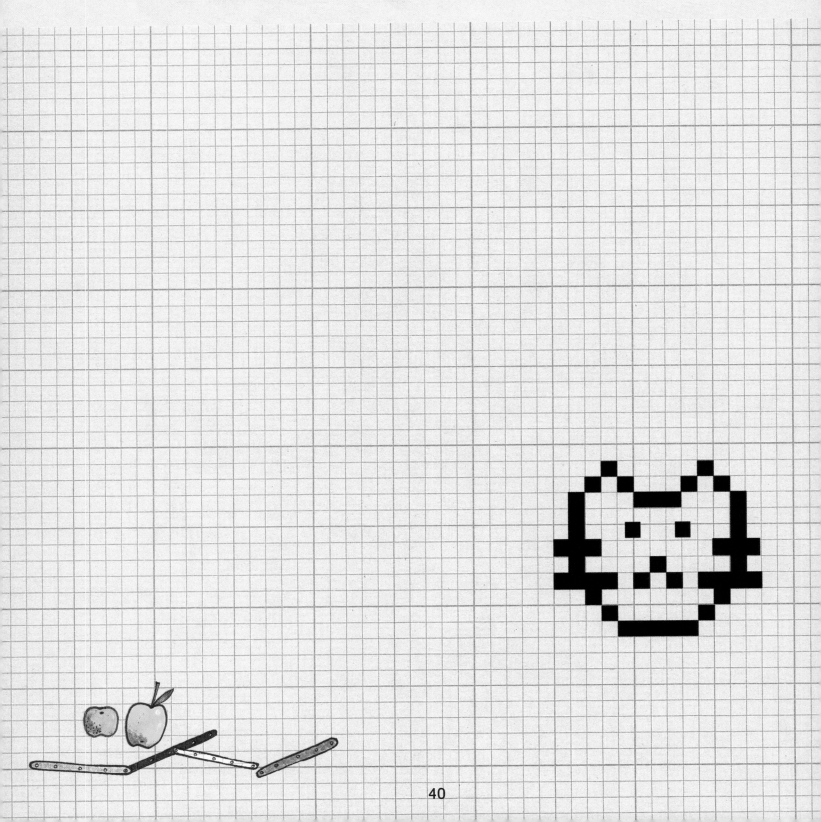

Don't use words like thin, thick, fat, or skinny. Say HOW thin, with a number.
Use the grid to count units of width or height. Use those units in your description.

Switch tasks and see if you can draw the object that your friend describes.

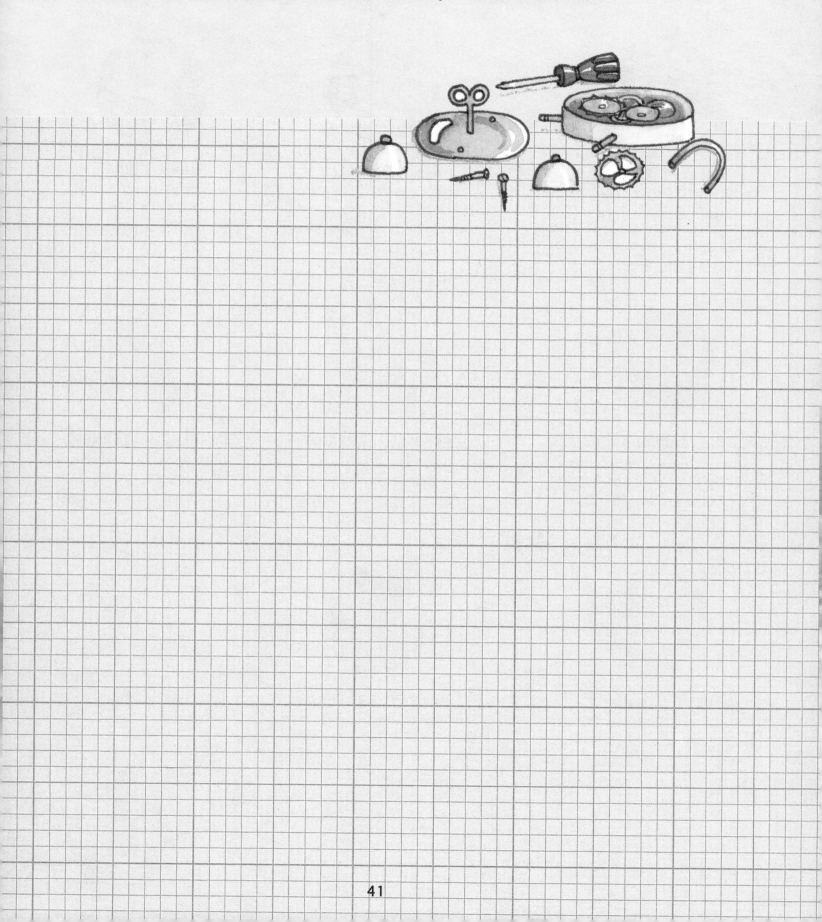

SCIENTISTS ARE UNIQUE.

Scientists look like this. Join the crowd!

HAYAT SINDI:
Science entrepreneur.
Brings affordable medical
tests to the world's
poorest people.

JANE GOODALL:
Wildlife researcher and
conservationist. Taught the
world about chimpanzees.

MARIE CURIE:
Physicist and chemist.
Two-time Nobel
Prize winner
(once in each field!).

MAGGIE ADERIN-POCOCK:
Space scientist and science
educator. Cohost of BBC
show *Sky at Night*.

STEPHEN HAWKING:
Theoretical physicist
and cosmologist.
Figured out black holes.

CHARLES H. TURNER:
Zoologist. Discovered
that insects can hear.

HEDY LAMARR:
Inventor and Hollywood movie
star. Invented the technology
that led to cell phones.

WANGARI MAATHAI:
Environmentalist and founder
of the Green Belt Movement.
In Kenya, the group has planted
10,000,000 (ten million) trees
to prevent erosion.

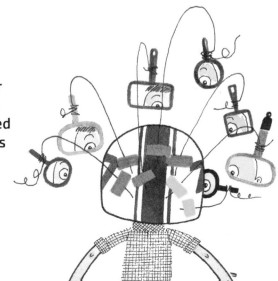

Draw a picture of yourself in the space provided below. Then write your future scientific accomplishment.

SCIENTISTS LEARN FROM OTHERS.

"If I have seen a little further than others, it is by standing upon the shoulders of giants." —Sir Isaac Newton

He described the universal theory of gravity and the laws of motion.

We each know things because of people who came before us.
Draw a picture of something you learned from someone else.

Now imagine they had not taught you. How would you figure it out by yourself?
Draw a picture of how you might do that:

SCIENTISTS LOOK AT THINGS IN NEW WAYS.

Look at the branches of this tree. Do you see any patterns or familiar shapes in the branches? Use your imagination. Outline or color shapes you find with a colored pencil. Now, turn the book upside down and look again. Do you see any images? Any patterns?

Make your own pattern finder. Randomly scribble on this page.
Now, look for patterns in your scribbles. Do you see faces?
Animals? Objects?

WHAT DOES IT MATTER?

Stuff in the universe that takes up space is called matter.
Anything you can touch, see, smell, or taste is made of matter.

Imagine that the universe is an enormous bowl of vegetable soup.
Yum. Universe soup!

What is that soup made of?

It has potatoes, carrots, beans, peas, and water.
(It does not have Brussels sprouts because everybody knows that
Brussels sprouts are awful in soup.)

Each vegetable can be broken down into "ingredients" such as carbohydrates, proteins, fiber, and water.

But what are *those* ingredients made of?

We can break each of them into tinier and tinier ingredients. Eventually, they get broken down to their most basic ingredients and can't be broken down any further. Stuff that is made of just one type of ingredient is an element.

CARBOHYDRATES

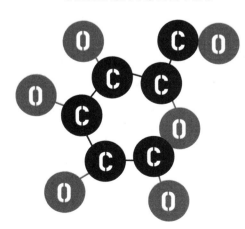

WATER

AMINO ACIDS

Side Chain

The official definition of an element is a substance that cannot be broken down by chemicals into simpler substances.

Elements can be broken down into smaller parts, but they are just parts and are no longer elements. Just like a tomato peel is part of the tomato but not a tomato. The parts of an element are ridiculously tiny. However, they have very groovy names like protons, electrons, neutrons, quarks, leptons, and hadrons. These names would probably make great rock 'n' roll band names!

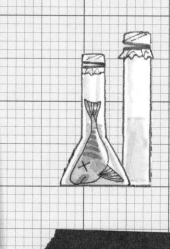

Chemistry investigates matter and its properties and how elements combine to form new substances.

Look at the things around you right now. Pick one and draw it here.

Can it be broken into smaller "ingredients"? If so, draw them here. What about those ingredients? Do they have ingredients, too? List or draw them here.

IT'S ELEMENTARY, MY DEAR!

One single item of an element is called an atom.

Atoms bond (stick) to other atoms to create molecules. Those other atoms can be the same element, or different.

A hydrogen molecule is 2 hydrogen atoms (H_2).

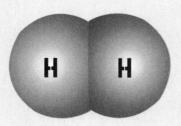

An oxygen molecule is 2 oxygen atoms (O_2).

A water molecule combines 2 hydrogen atoms and 1 oxygen atom (H_2O)

HERE ARE THE FORMULAS OF SOME OTHER COMMON MOLECULES THAT YOU ENCOUNTER:

CARBON DIOXIDE—You breathe this out when you exhale:
1 carbon atom and 2 oxygen atoms (CO_2)

SODIUM CHLORIDE—Table salt: 1 sodium atom and
1 chlorine atom ($NaCl$)

ACETIC ACID—Vinegar: 2 carbon atoms, 4 hydrogen atoms,
and 2 oxygen atoms ($C_2H_4O_2$)

SODIUM BICARBONATE—Baking soda, which makes cookies
and bread rise: 1 sodium atom, 1 hydrogen atom, 1 carbon atom,
and 3 oxygen atoms ($NaHCO_3$)

OBSERVE A CHEMICAL REACTION

MATERIALS

Large measuring cup

Vinegar (acetic acid)

Measuring spoons

Baking soda (sodium bicarbonate)

Pen or pencil (to make notes)

4. Put the measuring cup in the empty sink.

5. Measure out 1 tablespoon (approximately 15 ml) of baking soda.

6. Drop the baking soda into the vinegar.

7. Observe what happens. Make notes below.

_____

_____

_____

_____

_____

_____

1. Place a large measuring cup on the kitchen counter.

2. Pour vinegar into the measuring cup until you have 100 ml.

3. Observe the vinegar and make notes below.

_____

_____

_____

_____

8. Let it sit for 2 minutes, then observe again. Make notes.

_____

_____

_____

Record what you see, hear, and smell here. Do not drink or taste the mixture.

When you add the baking soda to the vinegar, the mixture will instantly bubble and rise rapidly in the measuring cup. Listen for the snap of bursting bubbles. How long does the fizzing last?

Is there the same amount of liquid in the measuring cup after the experiment as there was before? Does it look different?

Here's what's happening: The acetic acid ($C_2H_4O_2$) and sodium bicarbonate ($NaHCO_3$) recombine and form a new mixture of sodium acetate ($NaC_2H_3O_2$), water (H_2O), and carbon dioxide (CO_2). Carbon dioxide is a gas that rises out of the mixture and is released into the atmosphere as the bubbles burst.

An equation is a scientific description of what happens when molecules combine or separate. Here's a picture of the equation.

| $C_2H_4O_2$ | + | $NaHCO_3$ | $\longrightarrow$ | $NaC_2H_3O_2$ | + | H_2O | + | CO_2 |
| Acetic Acid | | Sodium Bicarbonate | | Sodium Acetate | | Water | | Carbon Dioxide |

KEY: ■ OXYGEN (O) ■ HYDROGEN (H) ■ CARBON (C) ■ SODIUM (Na)

A VERY BIG IDEA

A scientific law is a big rule about the universe that has been repeatedly shown through experiments to be true. One scientific law is the Law of Conservation of Mass and Energy.

The Law of Conservation of Mass and Energy says that mass and energy cannot be created or destroyed. They can be moved around or change forms, but they never disappear.

Matter is the physical stuff that takes up space in the universe. It includes anything you can see, touch, taste, feel, or move.

Mass is the amount of matter in an object. The mass of an object depends on the type of atoms and how many are packed into it.

Energy is the ability to do work or move things. There are two kinds of energy: potential and kinetic. Potential energy is stored and can be released and used when needed. Think of batteries, granola bars, or gasoline. Each contains stored energy.

Kinetic energy comes from the motion of waves, electrons, atoms, substances, or other objects. Think about the radiant energy of light from the sun or the heat energy from volcanoes or the movement of wind.

Think about the chemical reaction you created using vinegar and baking soda.

It started with 14 atoms and ended with the same 14 atoms.

It started with two kinds of molecules and ended with three completely different molecules. The reaction didn't make or destroy any atoms, it just moved them around to make new molecules.

There were 100 ml of liquid to begin with, but much less after. The molecules that had been in the vinegar broke apart and the atoms were rearranged into different molecules. Some of those molecules made bubbles of gas that popped as they reached the surface of the mixture and then floated away.

There seemed to be less stuff (matter) at the end of the experiment than in the beginning, but it all still exists. It is just in different forms. Some of it is floating around in the air as a gas instead of sitting inside the measuring cup as a liquid.

Count the atoms before the reaction and after the reaction. They are all still there! They have been kept (conserved).

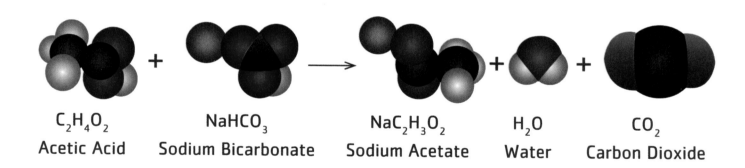

| $C_2H_4O_2$ | $NaHCO_3$ | $NaC_2H_3O_2$ | H_2O | CO_2 |
| Acetic Acid | Sodium Bicarbonate | Sodium Acetate | Water | Carbon Dioxide |

ATOMS BEFORE THE REACTION

2 + 1 carbon (C) atoms

4 + 1 hydrogen (H) atoms

2 + 3 oxygen (O) atoms

1 sodium (Na) atom

14 atoms total

ATOMS AFTER THE REACTION

2 + 1 carbon (C) atoms

3 + 2 hydrogen (H) atoms

2 + 1 + 2 oxygen (O) atoms

1 sodium (Na) atom

14 atoms total

DO THE ATOMIC SHUFFLE

Use these "atoms" to build a completely new shape. Make sure you use them all!
Remember, you can't create or destroy mass. You can only rearrange it!

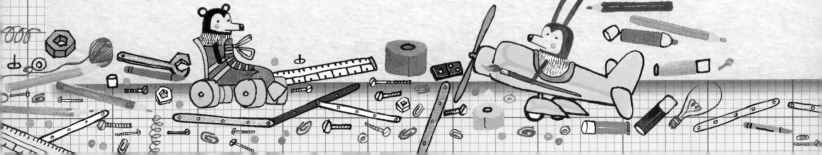

Draw your new creation here:

PLANTS

Plants contain a green chemical called chlorophyll that uses the energy of the sun to power a chemical reaction. That reaction combines CO_2 from the air and H_2O that is gathered by the roots of the plant into O_2 and a complex molecule called glucose ($C_6H_{12}O_6$). Glucose is a form of sugar. Plants use glucose for energy and save some in their stalks, roots, leaves, and fruits.

These are plant cells with chlorophyll. Chlorophyll absorbs the sun's energy to power a chemical reaction. Chlorophyll does not change during the chemical reaction, but it acts as a catalyst, speeding up the reaction.

ENERGY

CHLOROPHYLL

Absorbs the sun's energy to fuel the chemical reaction.

OXYGEN (O_2)

CARBON DIOXIDE (CO_2)

GLUCOSE ($C_6H_{12}O_6$)

- Some used for energy of plant growth.
- Some stored in leaves, roots, and fruits.

WATER (H_2O)

GROWING PLANTS

Watch a seed sprout.

MATERIALS

Paper towels

Empty baking dish

12 seeds each of 3 different types

Measuring cup

Water

Magnifying glass

Pen or pencil (to make notes)

1. Fold 2 sheets of paper towel in half and stack them in the bottom of the baking dish to form a layer four paper towel sheets thick.

2. Place 12 individual seeds of the first type on one third of the paper towel, leaving a space of 0.5–1 cm between the seeds.

3. Repeat with the other two types of seeds.

4. Fold another sheet of paper towel in half and use it to cover the seeds.

5. Measure 200 ml of water.

6. Pour the water evenly over the paper towels to moisten everything thoroughly.

7. Twice daily, peel back the top layer of paper towels. Use the magnifying glass to carefully observe the seeds. Record your observations here.

_____

_____

_____

_____

_____

_____

_____

8. Add water as needed to keep the paper towels moist. Continue checking and observing for at least fifteen days. Refer to the seed packet to learn about expected sprouting time for each type of seed.

_____

_____

_____

_____

_____

GROWING PLANTS

Grow seeds in soil.

MATERIALS

Empty paper egg carton

Tray or baking sheet

Potting soil mix

4 seeds each of 3 different types

3 Post-it notes (optional)

3 toothpicks (optional)

Pen or pencil

Water

1. Place the egg carton on a tray or baking sheet.

2. Fill each cavity three-quarters full of potting soil mix.

3. Place 1 seed of the first type in each of four cavities.

4. Cover each seed lightly with additional soil.

5. Repeat with the remaining seed types and egg carton cavities.

6. Make labels for each set of seeds by folding Post-it notes around the toothpicks. Write the names of one type of seed on each label. Put a label in one of the cavities holding that type of seed. Or you can write the name of each type of seed on the cover of the egg carton instead.

7. Water the seeds daily or as needed to keep the soil in the carton moist.

8. Observe the changes daily. Keep checking and observing for at least fifteen days. Refer to the seed packet to learn about the expected sprouting time for each type of seed. (If your seeds grow mold and do not sprout, throw them away and repeat the entire experiment with a new packet of seeds.)

9. Record your observations here.

_____

_____

_____

_____

After the seedlings sprout and grow to 4 cm tall, you can transplant them. To do so, prepare a flower pot with potting soil or dig a spot in the garden. Tear or cut the egg crate apart gently, separating each cavity. Pinch off the paper at the bottom of the egg carton so it is easy for the roots to grow. Place the bit of carton with each seedling into flower pots or your garden. Take care not to disturb the roots of your seedlings. Cover each with 2 cm of soil. Continue watering them regularly as they grow!

Continue making notes as your plants grow. What do you observe?

_____

_____

_____

Some varieties of seedlings transplant well, but others do not. Which variety of seeds grew best after transplanting?

PLANTS OBEY THE LAW.

Remember the Law of Conservation of Mass and Energy, which says that mass and energy cannot be created or destroyed, but can only be conserved?

The photosynthesis reaction conserves the carbon, oxygen, and hydrogen atoms. But it also conserves the energy!

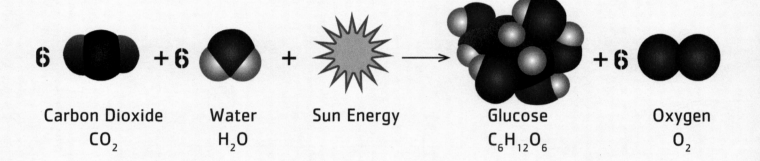

| Carbon Dioxide CO_2 | Water H_2O | Sun Energy | Glucose $C_6H_{12}O_6$ | Oxygen O_2 |

ATOM COUNT BEFORE PHOTOSYNTHESIS

6 carbon (C) atoms

6 x 2 oxygen (O) atoms +
6 oxygen (O) atoms

6 x 2 hydrogen (H) atoms

36 atoms total

ATOM COUNT AFTER PHOTOSYNTHESIS

6 carbon (C) atoms

6 oxygen (O) atoms +
6 x 2 oxygen (O) atoms

12 hydrogen (H) atoms

36 atoms total

The energy is stored in a special kind of sugar molecule called glucose and stays there until it is released by another chemical reaction called respiration.

When we eat plants, our body performs this chemical reaction and uses the released energy to grow and work and play!

That's why we eat plants!

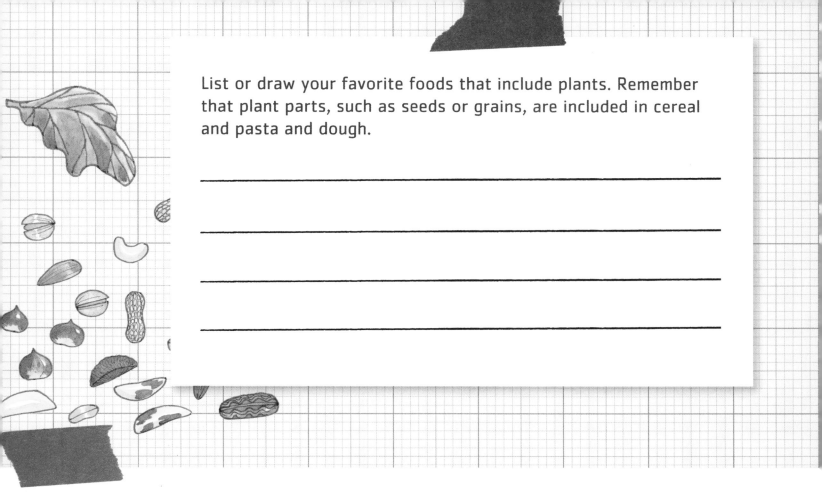

List or draw your favorite foods that include plants. Remember that plant parts, such as seeds or grains, are included in cereal and pasta and dough.

_____

_____

_____

_____

Draw a picture of you using plant energy to play or work:

ROTTEN PEACHES AND RESPIRATION

The respiration reaction looks like this:

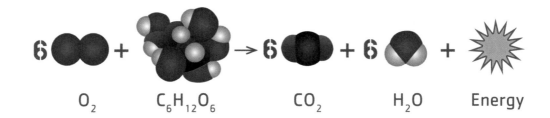

$$6\ O_2 + C_6H_{12}O_6 \rightarrow 6\ CO_2 + 6\ H_2O + \text{Energy}$$

Your body uses the energy from respiration to grow
and work and play.

You are not alone! Microorganisms, animals, fungi,
and plants also break apart glucose and release energy
through respiration.

The respiration reaction also happens when a plant dies.

Imagine a peach dropping from a tree onto the ground.
Will it look the same after a day? A week? A month?

Almost immediately, mold, fungus, insects, and animals begin the
work of breaking down the peach. It might take a long time,
but the peach will rot, and its elements will be released into the
ground. And through respiration, carbon dioxide
will return to the atmosphere.

WATCH IT ROT

1. Place the fruit in the yogurt container.

2. With the scissors, carefully cut a piece of plastic wrap large enough to cover the top of the yogurt container and to extend 5 cm over the edges.

3. Cover the top with the piece of plastic wrap and secure it with rubber bands.

4. Using the pencil, poke ten holes in the plastic wrap.

5. Place the container on a counter or table.

6. Observe daily for one month. Note changes to the size, shape, smell, color, and texture of the fruit. Do not taste the rotting fruit.

MATERIALS

1/4 of a peach, nectarine, or plum

Clean empty yogurt container

Plastic wrap

Scissors

Rubber bands

Sharp pencil

Record your notes here:

_____

_____

_____

_____

DECOMPOSERS

Can you help Ada Twist explore the forest floor?

In the autumn, bright red, orange, and gold leaves drop to the forest floor.
By spring, the leaves are brown, crumpled, and rotten. Ada wonders why.

Why don't the colorful leaves pile up, year after year, until the trees are
buried beneath them? Why do they turn brown?

WRITE YOUR IDEAS HERE:

_____

_____

_____

_____

Many organisms work to break down or decompose the
leaves and return their nutrients to the earth for plants
to use. These organisms are called decomposers.

Help Ada discover some of the organisms that do this
important job.

MATERIALS

White plastic garbage bag

Magnifying glass

Rubber gloves

Hand trowel

1. With an adult, find a place beneath the
   trees in a forest or garden where leaves
   are rotting.

2. Spread the garbage bag over the ground
   next to the area.

3. Use the magnifying glass to observe
   the leaves. Make notes about their
   color and texture.

4. Put on the rubber gloves. Use the trowel to scoop some rotting leaves onto the garbage bag. Spread the leaves around and use the magnifying glass again to observe any insects, worms, or other animals you find.

5. Dig another scoop from deeper in the leaves. Spread those on another part of the garbage bag.

6. Observe and record your observations.

7. Continue digging and observing.

8. Try different locations under different trees or near rotting logs. Are there other insects, worms, animals, or organisms?

Are the leaves different in shape, texture, size, smell, or color as you dig deeper in the pile? What else do you see? Are there roots? Mushrooms or other fungi? (NEVER eat any mushrooms or plants you find in the forest. And be sure to wash your hands and clothes after coming in contact with plants.)

Are there earthworms? Roly-poly bugs? Millipedes?

Use reference books from the library to identify the organisms that you find.

Draw pictures and write notes here:

THE CARBON CYCLE

Remember the Law of Conservation of Mass and Energy? Of course you do!

It says that mass and energy can't be created or destroyed, but can be rearranged. Here's an example: Nature rearranges carbon, hydrogen, and oxygen molecules during photosynthesis and respiration.

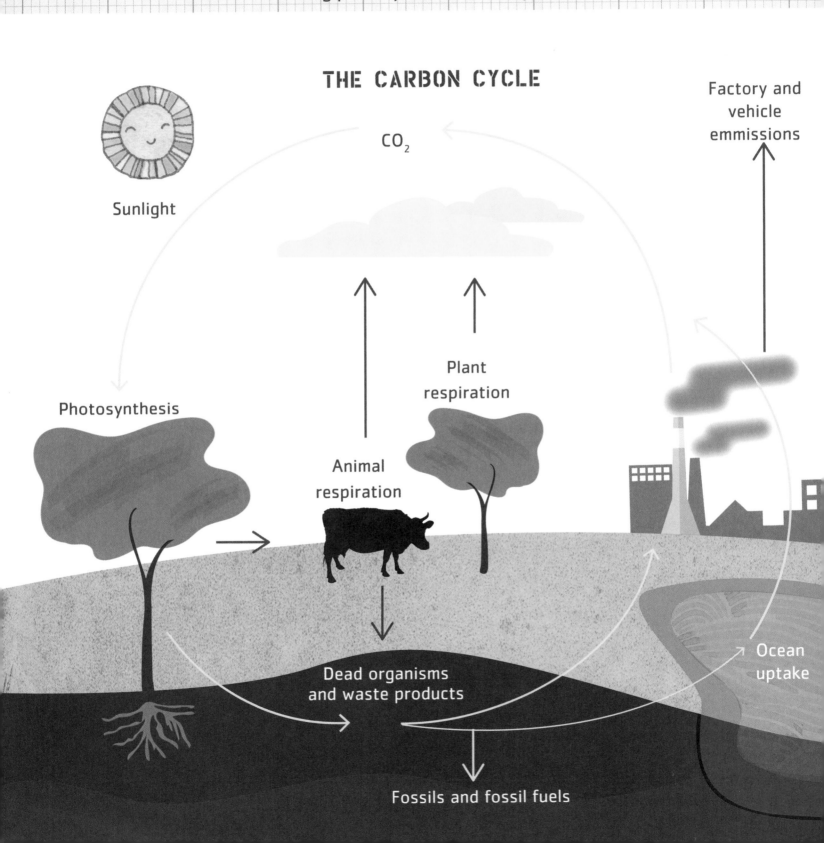

THE CARBON CYCLE

Sunlight

CO_2

Factory and vehicle emmissions

Photosynthesis

Plant respiration

Animal respiration

Ocean uptake

Dead organisms and waste products

Fossils and fossil fuels

Plants take in carbon dioxide and release oxygen.

Then decomposers take in oxygen and release carbon dioxide through respiration.

Then plants take in carbon dioxide and release oxygen into the atmosphere.

Then decomposers take in oxygen and release carbon dioxide.

Then plants take carbon dioxide and . . .

WAIT!

Is there an echo in here? Are you noticing a pattern?

Of course you are. The creation and use of carbon dioxide is going in a circle. This is called the carbon cycle.

The carbon cycle gives us oxygen to breathe and helps plants and animals rot when they die, which keeps our planet from being buried in unrotted leaves and animals! Imagine how deep the leaves in your yard would be if they piled up for millions of years. After all, trees have been growing on the earth for over 350 million years. That's a lot of years and a lot of leaves!

The carbon cycle constantly removes carbon dioxide from the air and returns oxygen. The chemical reactions do not change. However, the exact amounts of carbon dioxide and oxygen in the atmosphere change slowly over hundreds of thousands of years.

When carbon dioxide builds up in the atmosphere, the earth warms. When carbon dioxide diminishes in the atmosphere, the earth cools. These slow changes have contributed to warming periods and ice ages throughout history.

Scientists know this because they are detectives. Scientists have studied levels of carbon dioxide in ice samples from glaciers, ocean samples, tree cores, and other places. Scientists use this information and other data to show climate history.

WEATHER VS. CLIMATE

It is important to know the difference between weather and climate. Sometimes people point to a very cold day or a snowstorm and say that the earth is not warming. They are confusing weather and climate.

Weather is how the atmosphere behaves over a short period of time. It includes things like air temperature, wind direction and speed, rain or snow or other precipitation, and atmospheric pressure.

Climate is the weather pattern of a particular area over a relatively long amount of time—at least thirty years, according to the National Aeronautics and Space Administration (NASA), though climate data over a much longer period is used when it is available.

Use this chart to keep track of the weather where you live for one week. Gather the information from the local newspaper or news station. If you kept these records for many, many decades, you could get a picture of the climate where you live.

	MONDAY		TUESDAY		WEDNESDAY		THURSDAY		FRIDAY		SATURDAY		SUNDAY	
	AM	PM	AM	PM	AM	PM	AM	PM	AM	PM	AM	PM	AM	PM
TIME														
TEMPERATURE														
WIND DIRECTION														
WIND SPEED														
PRECIPITATION														

Evidence shows that the earth's climate has gone through many changes throughout history. But something new and different is going on now. Something everyone needs to understand. Something dangerous!

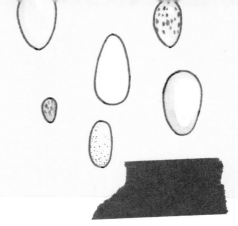

The earth's atmosphere is warming rapidly. The rate of change in temperature and carbon dioxide levels in our atmosphere is increasing at a drastic pace!

If it continues, the rise in temperature will have dangerous effects on the earth and all its inhabitants, including plants and animals. That includes us!

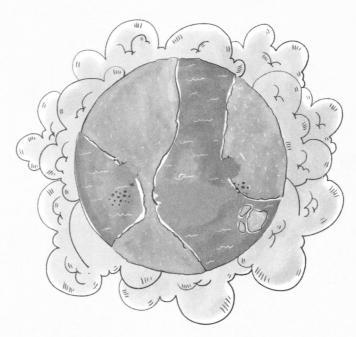

Why is this happening now?

The answer to this question began hundreds of millions of years ago.

Let's read a story about it! Get cozy! Perhaps enjoy a nice cookie and a glass of milk while you read. It's a very, very, veeeeerrryyyy slow story.

THE STORY OF BOB THE UNLUCKY LEAF

Once upon a time, 300 million years ago, the earth was covered with oceans and forested, swampy lands. It was awesome. And kind of creepy. But mostly awesome.

In a swampy forest, there was a leaf named Bob who clung to a tree. One day, Bob fell into the swamp. The end . . . of Bob. But not the end of our story. Actually, it wasn't even the end of Bob.

The swampy forests looked like this.

Bob got covered by water and dirt and other plants and animals that also fell into the mucky water. Normally, leaves (like Bob) and other organisms rot and release CO_2 into the atmosphere. However, Bob and the other organisms could not rot completely, because there was too little oxygen in the water for respiration. So they partially rotted in the stagnant waters and became peat. Peat is a spongy bunch of condensed, partially rotted dead stuff from a swamp. It's cool. And also kind of creepy. But mostly cool.

Days passed. Weeks passed. Months, years, and centuries went by. Bob got bored. But that's what happens when you are a partially rotted leaf in a big pile of leaves getting squished by all the other dead leaves and animals piling up above you.

Then suddenly . . . 300 million years passed. Phew. That was fast!

The weight of the plants and animals piling up over 300 million years put enormous pressure on the stuff at the bottom of the pile, including Bob. Eventually, pressure and heat led to chemical changes in the dead stuff.

Remember that leaves (like Bob) contain glucose molecules ($C_6H_{12}O_6$). Also remember that all the atoms in the glucose molecule can be moved around but never disappear because of the Law of Conservation of Mass and Energy. Some of Bob's carbon atoms were released as carbon dioxide, and some got stuck with hydrogen to create a gas called methane (CH_4). Others were squished under enormous heat and pressure and became coal. Coal is mostly made of carbon (C).

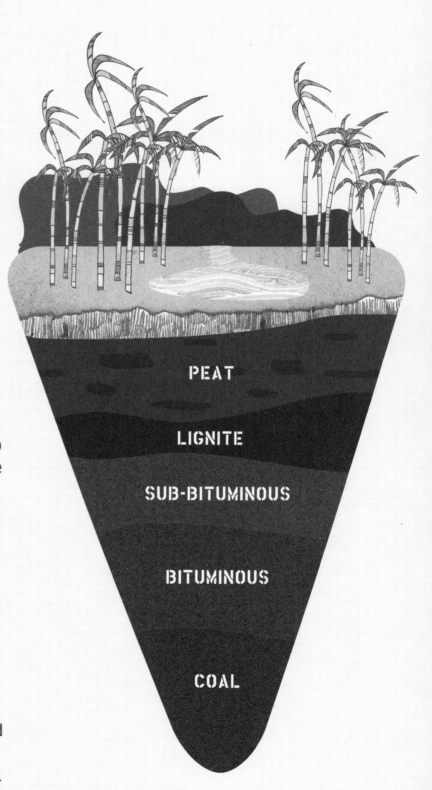

PEAT

LIGNITE

SUB-BITUMINOUS

BITUMINOUS

COAL

The animals and plankton and other organisms that died in the oceans during this time went through a similar process of high pressure and heat and became oil or natural gas, both of which are also loaded with carbon atoms.

All of this happened during a time that paleontologists call the Carboniferous period of our geological history. Vast pockets of oil, coal, and gas from this time are hidden deep beneath the surface of the earth and its oceans.

The energy that Bob and the other plants and animals stored as glucose was never released through respiration. It was conserved in the coal. That's why coal is a powerful energy source. Coal, oil, and natural gas contain the energy from the sun that went into the plants and the animals that ate the plants. Those dead plants and animals are called fossils, and coal, oil, and natural gas are called fossil fuels.

When fossil fuels combine with oxygen and are combusted or burned, they release heat energy and carbon dioxide.

We use that energy for electricity, cooking, heating our homes, and driving our cars. The carbon dioxide goes into the atmosphere, where it stays until a plant can use it for photosynthesis and the carbon cycle can begin again.

So, whatever happened to Bob?

He became part of a chunk of coal, which was burned in an electric plant to make electricity. And that really was the end of Bob.

And our story.

THE END.

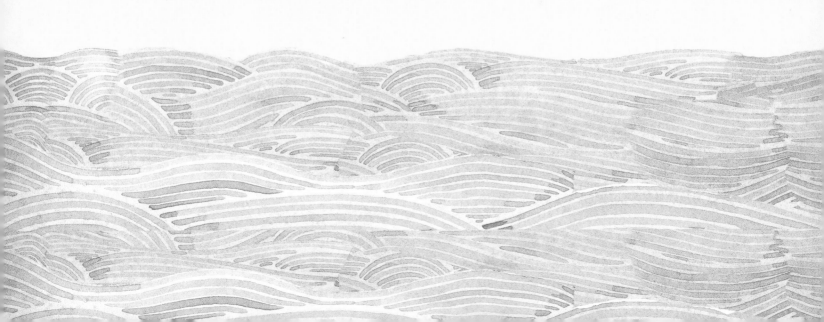

FOSSIL FUELS, OIL, AND COMBUSTION

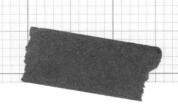

We mine and drill for fossil fuels and use them to power just about everything we do.

Coal and natural gas are used to make electricity.

Look around right now. What do you see that uses electricity?

List it here:

_____

_____

_____

_____

_____

_____

_____

Oil is turned into gasoline and used as fuel for cars and planes. Also, it is used to make plastics and other materials.

Look around. What do you see that is made of plastic or man-made fibers? (Natural fibers, found in nature, include cotton, flax, or bamboo.)

Make a list here:

_____

_____

_____

_____

_____

_____

_____

Combustion engines burn coal, oil, or gas to perform work or create electricity.

List machines you know that have engines:

_____

_____

_____

_____

_____

_____

_____

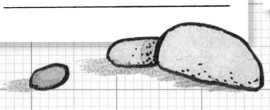

SO WHAT?

We use a lot of fossil fuels. The amount has gone up, up, up as we have invented and built more and more machines that burn gasoline or other fossil fuels.

Here's the problem. Burning fossil fuels pumps carbon dioxide molecules into the atmosphere. These molecules, along with water and methane molecules, let sunlight through to the earth.

The light warms the earth's surface. The earth sends heat toward space, but carbon dioxide (and other) molecules trap the heat in our atmosphere. The earth can't cool off. As more sunlight reaches the earth's surface, the earth gets warmer and warmer and warmer.

We call carbon dioxide and methane greenhouse gases because they let in light but trap heat, like the roof of a greenhouse.

Scientists have shown that the rate of warming of the earth's atmosphere is caused by mankind's increasing use of fossil fuels.

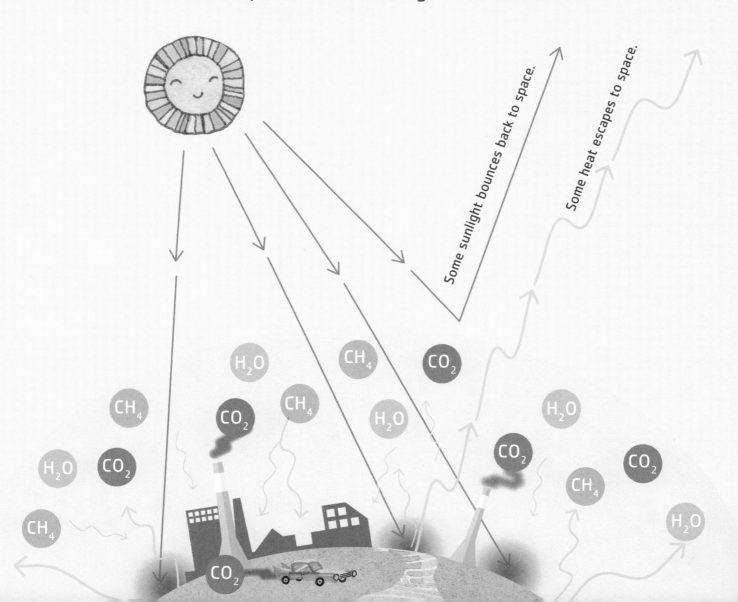

Gas-fueled cars and trucks are a major source of carbon dioxide in the atmosphere. Can you design a vehicle that uses wind energy or solar energy or some other renewable energy? Draw it here:

SO WHAT?

Why does it matter if CO_2 and other greenhouse gases build up in our atmosphere? Why does it matter that the earth's atmosphere is warming at an alarming rate?

RISING GLOBAL TEMPERATURES CAUSE:

- Changes in precipitation patterns. This affects crops and food supplies.

- Bigger, more frequent, and more intense hurricanes.

- Increased heat waves and droughts and fires.

- Arctic and Antarctic ice melts.

- Rising sea levels.
  - What will happen to the animals who live on the ice? Polar bears? Penguins?

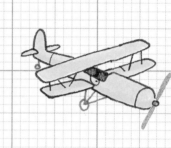

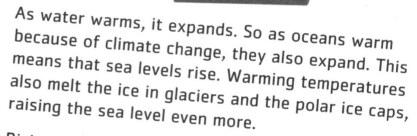

As water warms, it expands. So as oceans warm because of climate change, they also expand. This means that sea levels rise. Warming temperatures also melt the ice in glaciers and the polar ice caps, raising the sea level even more.

Rising sea levels put coastal cities at risk for flooding during storms.

About 40 percent of the world's population lives within 100 km of the coast. Millions of people will lose their homes to rising water. Where will those people go? How will they live?

- The destruction of the earth's rain forests is adding to the problem.

- Massive amounts of extra CO_2 are trapped in trees in the earth's rain forests. When these forests die, lots more CO_2 is released through respiration of the rotting trees or burning of the trees. When rain forests are cut or burned, the trees are not there to reabsorb the carbon dioxide in the atmosphere. This means even more carbon dioxide builds up in the atmosphere. More than 80 percent of the earth's natural forests have been destroyed since 1900.

Climate change is complicated. Climate change is also affected by ocean currents, wind patterns, and the release of greenhouse gases like methane.

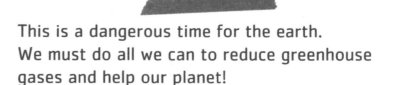

This is a dangerous time for the earth. We must do all we can to reduce greenhouse gases and help our planet!

Go to the library and research more about greenhouse gases and climate change. The more you know about it, the more you can do to help combat it!

THE ENERGY GAME

We can slow and, hopefully, reverse some of the effects of climate change if we act quickly. We must find and use renewable energy sources because they do not add greenhouse gases to the atmosphere. We must also decrease our energy use and protect the rain forests.

However, the time to act is short. As the earth warms, the effects of climate change become more intense and will eventually hit a level at which they cannot be reversed!

In this game, you must help us move from carbon-based fuels to clean energy sources, such as solar, wind, or wave power. You can also improve the situation by helping plant trees or finding new ways to reduce energy use.

Can you reach the end of the game before the earth overheats?

MATERIALS: 20 PENNIES, 1 DIME, 1 NICKEL

HOW TO PLAY:

1. Place pennies on the carbon (C) markers in the coal and oil fields. These are your fossil fuels.

2. Place your dime at the **START**.

3. Flip your nickel to determine the number of spaces you can move.

    a. Heads – Move one space

    b. Tails – Move two spaces

4. As you use fossil fuel, the carbon will combine with oxygen in the atmosphere and raise the temperature on the thermometer! Follow the instructions on the spaces where you land to move pennies to and from the thermometer. If the thermometer reaches the "Tipping Point," pennies cannot be removed, no matter what the squares on the board say.

5. Some actions (like inventing new energy efficient technologies or conserving resources) move pennies off the board. They are out of play. You have conserved them!

6. If you reach the **END** before the thermometer reaches the top, you win! If the earth overheats before you reach the end, we all lose!

7. Good luck! The earth is counting on you!

SUN

WIND

START

| City chooses diesel buses. Move 3 from fossil fuels. | AC set too low! Use too much electricity. Move 2 from fossil fuels. | New solar farm! Move 2 to the sun! | Not paying attention to climate change. Go back 2 spaces. | Leave computer on at night. Move 1 from fossil fuels. | New wind farm! Move 2 to wind! |

| No public transportation funds. Move 3 from fossil fuels. | Raise funds to help replant rain forests. Move 2 to rain forest. | Limit hot water use. Remove 1 from board. | School recycling program! Remove 1 from board. | Fuel efficiency law reversed. Move 4 from fossil fuels. | High fuel efficiency laws for autos! Remove 2 from board. |

| Walk, bike, or carpool to school. Remove 1 from board. | New solar farm. Move 2 to sun. | New high-efficiency battery invented! Remove 1 from board. | Ocean waves power factory. Move 2 to ocean. | Palm oil banned. Rain forest saved. Move 2 to rain forest. | Better public transportation. Remove 2 from board. |

RAIN FOREST

END

| Find way to educate adults on climate change. Move 1 each to sun, wind, ocean, and rain forest. | Environmental laws weakened. Move 4 from fossil fuels. |

OCEAN

C C
C C C
C C C C C
COAL
C C
C C C C C C C C

OIL

TIPPING POINT

BY THE SEA!

Each summer, Ada and her family vacation on the coast with her grandparents. They visit a small island, where Ada hunts for answers to her many questions while her brother hunts for treasure.

They built a driftwood fort three years ago on a hill near the center of the island. On every visit, they comb the beach and add to their science/pirate fort.

This year, Ada and her brother were shocked when they got to the island. The fort was gone! A hurricane had pushed a powerful wall of water onto the island and swept the fort away.

Ada did not understand. The fort was high above the beach and far from the shore. How could waves reach it?

After vacation, she did some research, and she learned that sea levels are rising due to climate change. The warming atmosphere also causes stronger and more frequent hurricanes. These strong storms push enormous amounts of water in front of them. This is called a storm surge. Storm surges can be many meters high and flood lands far from the shore. This kind of flooding affects millions of people around the world and will get worse as the climate continues to warm. Storm surges over 8 meters high have been recorded!

Ada also learned about topographical maps. They show how high the land is above sea level. Help Ada use a topographical map to find a safe place for her next fort.

Each ring of the map shows the height of the land above sea level. The distance between rings shows how quickly the land slopes up or down.

Rings that are far apart show that the land is not steep. Rings that are very close together show a steep hill.

Using your colored pencils, show where the water would flood on Ada's Island if the storm surge is:

3D MAP KEY: 2 METERS   3 METERS   4 METERS   **5 METERS**   6 METERS

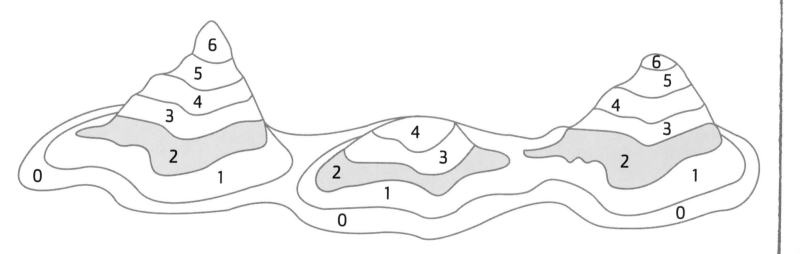

Where should Ada and her brother build their next fort? Draw it on their science/pirate map. Add a watchtower, and mark three spots to bury treasure. What else could they build?

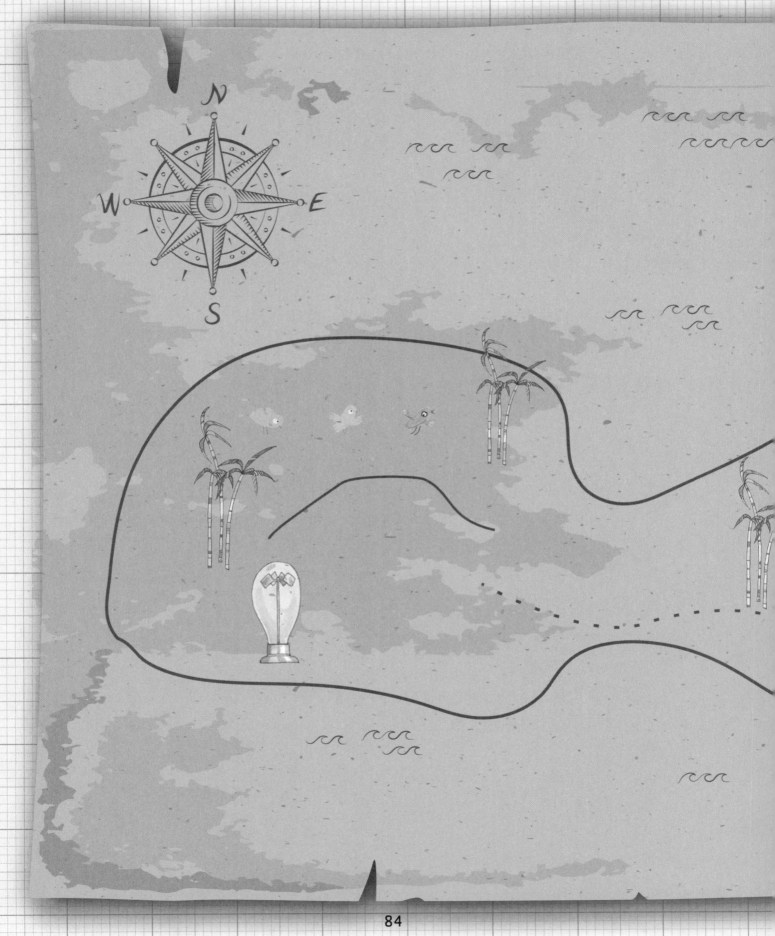

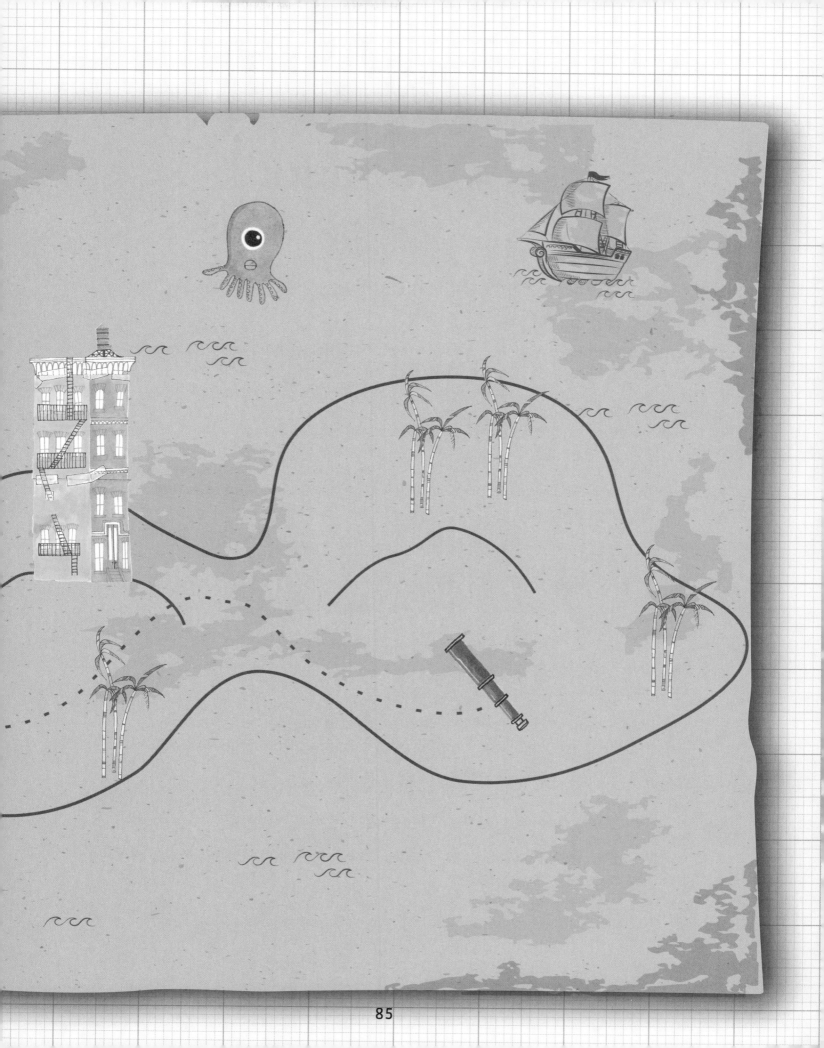

WHAT CAN YOU DO TO HELP REDUCE THE CO₂ IN THE ATMOSPHERE?

HERE ARE 10 THINGS YOU AND YOUR FAMILY CAN DO
STARTING RIGHT NOW:

1. Reduce your energy consumption: Turn off lights and power off electronics when not using them. Unplug the electronics or use a power strip to completely cut power when they are not being used.

2. Change your travel habits: Bike, walk, or use public transportation when possible instead of being driven. Carpool with friends if you have to drive.

3. RECYCLE and REUSE! This prevents the need for new manufacturing. Shop at thrift stores.

4. Buy products with less packaging.

5. Change your food habits: Support local food growers by shopping at a farmers' market. This reduces carbon emissions from shipping. Even better . . . grow your own garden!

6. Ask your parents to set the thermostat a little cooler in winter and wear sweaters inside.

7. Ask your parents to set the thermostat a little warmer in summer. Dress cooler. Use fans instead of air conditioning when you can.

8. Take showers instead of baths to use less hot water.

9. Get a reusable, refillable bottle for water instead of buying bottled water.

10. Cut down on laundry and water heater usage by using clothes and towels multiple times before laundering.

5 BIG ACTIONS

5 BIG ACTIONS WE MUST ALL TAKE:

1. Encourage replanting of forests globally.

2. Transition to renewable and carbon-neutral energy sources such as solar and wind power.

3. Contact community, national, and world leaders to demand they work to battle climate change.

4. Educate others about the fight to save our planet from climate change.

5. Support businesses that fight climate change.

MORE ACTION ITEMS:

Start with research. The library is the perfect place to get started.
Work with the librarian to learn about these topics. Think about how you
can make a difference with that information.

STARTING POINTS:

1. Learn about global organizations that fight climate change.

2. Learn about global organizations that replant depleted forests around the world.

3. Who are your government officials? What are their records on climate policy? Contact them and tell them what you think is important!

Get other kids involved, too! The future is up to you!

SCIENTISTS ARE PATIENT.

Science is a process of asking questions and looking for answers by doing tests called experiments. Some experiments take a long time. One of the longest experiments in history took almost 70 years. It was begun in 1944. Scientists in Dublin, Ireland, had evidence that tar pitch (the material used for many roads) would form a drop, but they had never observed it happening. They created a simple experiment to see, but the tar-pitch was veeeeeerrrrrrry slooooooooooooooooooooooooooooooooow. Finally, in 2013, a drop was recorded on camera!

Imagine if you did an experiment that took 70 years before you finally got your answer. Draw a picture of older you celebrating 70 years from now! How old would you be?

SCIENTISTS ARE PERSISTENT.

They don't give up when things go wrong.

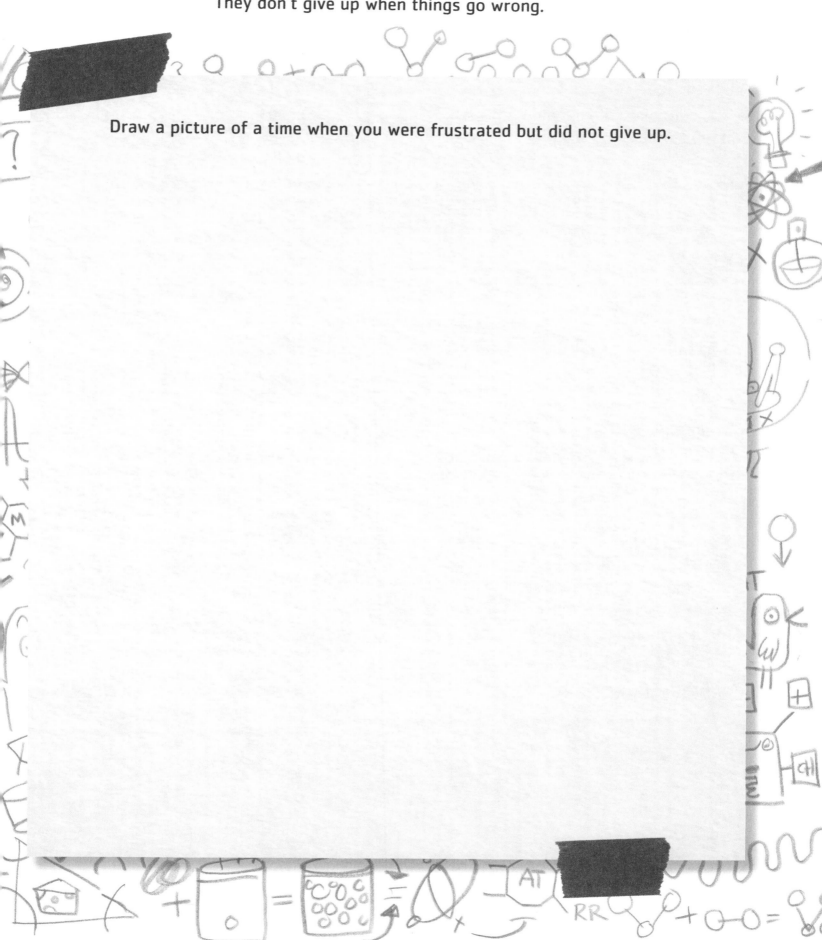

Draw a picture of a time when you were frustrated but did not give up.

GLOSSARY

ATMOSPHERE

A layer of gases surrounding a planet and held in place by the planet's gravity. The earth's atmosphere is about 78 percent nitrogen, 21 percent oxygen, and the rest is a mix of argon, carbon dioxide, and other gases.

ATOM

The smallest component of an element that shares the chemical properties of that element. An atom is made of smaller particles including neutrons, protons, and electrons.

CARBON CYCLE

The cycle in which carbon moves from the earth to the atmosphere and back again through a series of chemical reactions.

CATALYST

A substance that speeds up a chemical reaction but is not used up by the reaction. For instance, if cleaning your room was a chemical reaction, your frowning mom in the doorway would make you clean it faster— she would be a catalyst!

CHEMICAL REACTION

A process that changes or transforms one set of chemicals into another.

CHLOROPHYLL

A green substance in algae and plants that absorbs energy from light. Chlorophyll is a catalyst in the photosynthesis reaction.

CLIMATE

The weather over long periods of time. It includes information on wind, temperature, humidity, precipitation, and other data relating to weather.

CLIMATE CHANGE

Long-lasting changes in weather patterns. These patterns can last for periods from decades to millions of years.

COMBUSTION

The process of burning a substance. Combustion combines the substance with oxygen and produces heat and light.

CONSTELLATION

A group of stars that form a pattern that people consider to represent mythological creatures or people, animals, or other meaningful images.

DATA

Individual pieces of information.

DECOMPOSERS

The organisms that break down dead or rotting plants and animals.

ELECTRON

Part of an atom. An electron is a particle with a negative electrical charge. The proton and neutron form the nucleus of the atom, and the electrons orbit around the nucleus.

ELEMENT

A substance made of only one type of atom.

ENERGY

The power—from heat, light, or motion—to do work.

EQUATION

A way of writing what happens in a chemical reaction. The left side of an equation shows the beginning molecules. The right side of an equation shows the molecules after the reaction.

FACT

Something that is proven true with evidence.

FOSSIL FUELS

Fuels such as oil, coal, or methane, which are formed over millions of years by the decomposition of buried dead plants and animals. They are rich in carbon and high in energy.

FOSSILS

The remains of once-living things from over 10,000 years ago.

FRICTION

The force that slows down the movement of one object sliding against another.

GLUCOSE

A simple sugar compound made during photosynthesis from carbon dioxide and water. Glucose molecules have six carbon atoms bonded to twelve hydrogen atoms and six oxygen atoms. The formula looks like this: $C_6H_{12}O_6$. Glucose is a basic source of energy for most living things on earth.

GRAVITY

A force that pulls together all matter. Gravity increases as the amount of matter increases. For instance, the sun, which has an enormous amount of matter, has enough gravity to attract the planets in our solar system and keep them in its orbit. The earth's gravity keeps us from floating into space.

GREENHOUSE GAS

A chemical compound that absorbs and traps radiation from the sun and holds heat in the atmosphere.

HYPOTHESIS

A suggested explanation for something that happens and which can be tested. A hypothesis is based on previous observations.

LAW OF CONSERVATION OF MASS AND ENERGY

The amount of matter and energy available in the universe cannot be created or destroyed. Matter and energy can be moved and changed, but the amount remains the same.

MASS

The amount of matter in an object.

MATTER

Anything that takes up space and has mass.

MEASURE

To determine the amount or size of something by comparing it to an object of known size.

METEOR

A small rocky or metallic object that is heated by friction as it enters the earth's atmosphere and appears as a streak of light in the sky.

MOLECULE

Two or more atoms that form a chemical bond together. The atoms can be of the same element or different elements.

NEUTRON

Part of an atom. A neutron is a particle with no electrical charge. Protons and neutrons form the nucleus of the atom, and electrons orbit around the nucleus.

NUCLEUS

The center part of an atom made of protons and neutrons. Electrons orbit around the nucleus.

OBSERVE

To carefully watch and notice something.

ORIGIN

The source or point at which something begins.

OXYGEN

An odorless, tasteless, and colorless gas which is used by animals and plants during respiration. Oxygen makes up about 21 percent of the earth's atmosphere.

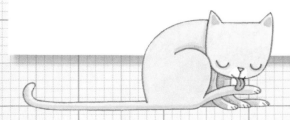

PHOTOSYNTHESIS

A process in which plants use the energy from sunlight to make food from water and carbon dioxide and release oxygen into the atmosphere.

PLASMA

The state of matter that occurs when energy is added to a gas so that some of its electrons leave its atoms.

PRECIPITATION

Moisture in the form of snow, rain, sleet, or hail that falls to the ground.

PROTON

Part of an atom. A proton is a particle with a positive electrical charge.

SCIENTIFIC METHOD

A set of steps used by scientists to investigate something:

1. Make an observation.

2. Ask a question.

3. Form an explanation that can be tested—this is called a hypothesis.

4. Predict what will happen based on the hypothesis.

5. Test the prediction.

6. Repeat the steps using the results to make and test new hypotheses.

STAR

A huge sphere of very hot, glowing plasma that is held together by its own gravity. Our sun is a star.

TOPOGRAPHICAL MAP

A map showing the shape of the ground.

WANING MOON

A moon which appears to be decreasing in size as it moves from the full moon to the new moon.

WAXING MOON

A moon which appears to be increasing in size as it moves from the new moon to the full moon.

WEATHER

The daily conditions of the atmosphere such as precipitation, wind, temperature, and atmospheric pressure.

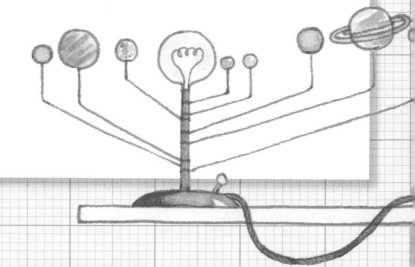

SOLUTION TO SCIENTIST'S WORD SEARCH

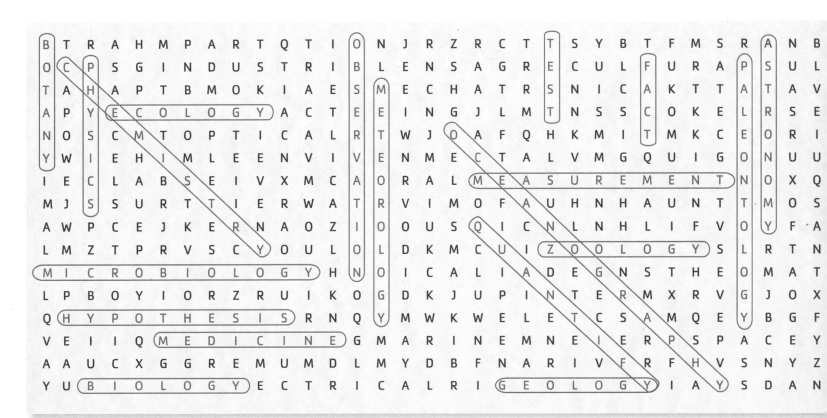

BOTANY	OCEANOGRAPHY	MICROBIOLOGY	OBSERVATION
BIOLOGY	ASTRONOMY	PALEONTOLOGY	MEASUREMENT
CHEMISTRY	METEOROLOGY	ECOLOGY	QUANTIFY
PHYSICS	ZOOLOGY	HYPOTHESIS	FACT
GEOLOGY	MEDICINE	TEST	